alōōza readers

BegR
Black
8.20.07
NEW

EMERGING
2
READER

Salty, Sandy, Soggy Homes

By Susan Blackaby

School Specialty® Publishing

Text Copyright © 2007 School Specialty Publishing. Manatee Character © 2003 by John Lithgow. Manatee Illustration © 2003 by Ard Hoyt.

Printed in the United States of America. All rights reserved. Except as permitted under the United States Copyright Act, no part of this publication may be reproduced or distributed in any form or by any means, or stored in a database or retrieval system, without prior written permission from the publisher, unless otherwise indicated.

Library of Congress Cataloging-in-Publication Data is on file with the publisher.

Send all inquiries to:
School Specialty Publishing
8720 Orion Place
Columbus, OH 43240-2111

ISBN 0-7696-4242-X

1 2 3 4 5 6 7 8 9 10 PHXBK 12 11 10 09 08 07 06

NORTH LOGAN CITY LIBRARY
475 East 2500 North
North Logan, UT 84341
435-755-7169

Hi, I'm a manatee.
Join me in learning about
animals that live in water habitats.
All animals need water.
Some live near the water.
Some live on the water.
Some animals—like me—live in the water.
Find out about these soggy homes
and the animals that live there.

Table of Contents

The Ocean

Look at the earth from space.
It looks like a blue ball.
The blue parts on the earth are water.
Saltwater oceans cover most
of the planet.
The world's largest animals live
in the ocean.
The world's smallest animals live
there, too.

Most **marine** animals stay
underwater all of the time.
They breathe through **gills**.
The ocean gives them food and shelter.
Fish, eels, and sharks swim day in
and day out.
So do jellyfish, squid, and sea horses.

Marine **mammals** do not have gills.
They cannot breathe under the water.
Dolphins and whales dive deep
to find food.
Then, they must come up for air.

The Shoreline

Waves crash on the **shoreline**.
This is where the ocean meets the land.
Some animals live on land
and in water.
Turtles lay eggs in the sand.
Then, they swim back out to sea.
Sea lions and seals splash in the water.
Then, they lay on the beach.

Tide Pool

A **tide pool** is a rocky hole.
It fills with water when the **tide**
is high.
It traps seawater.
It traps sea animals.
Starfish and sea urchins live
in tide pools.
So do mussels, crabs, and snails.

Estuary

An **estuary** is where a river meets the ocean.
It has land on two or three sides of it.
In an estuary, freshwater mixes with salt water.
Oysters live in estuaries.
Fish, crabs, and lobsters live there, too.

NORTH LOGAN CITY LIBRARY
475 East 2500 North
North Logan, UT 84341
435-755-7169

Swamp

A **swamp** is a low piece of land
usually covered by water.
Trees and shrubs grow in it.
Mangrove trees grow in swamps.
Manatees live in the warm, salty water.
So do crocodiles.

Salt Marsh

A salt **marsh** is a space between
salt water and land.
The salty water is not deep.
The water moves very slowly.
Birds come to a salt marsh to find food.
Herons step through the water.
They eat the bugs and fish they find.

Freshwater Marsh

A marsh can also be near freshwater.
The water there is not salty.
Grasses and flowers grow in it.
The water is not deep.
Ducks and geese live there.
Turtles live there, too.

River

Rain falls.
It soaks into the ground.
It also runs over the ground
into a stream.
Small streams join together.
They make a river.
Small rivers join together.
They make big rivers.
Rivers carry water to the ocean.

Some rivers run fast.
Some rivers run slowly.
Fish, turtles, and snakes live in rivers.
Birds nest on the **banks**.
Raccoons, river otters, and bears
hunt for food in rivers.

Pond and Lake

A pond is a small body of water.
The water in a pond does not move.
A lake is a large body of water.
Ponds and lakes have land
all around them.

Most ponds and lakes are
freshwater **habitats**.
Bass, carp, and trout live there.
Frogs, newts, and salamanders
live there.
Muskrats build homes there
out of weeds and mud.
Ponds and lakes are two of the many
soggy places that animals call home.

Vocabulary

bank–the ground bordering a stream, river, or lake. *The duck hid in the grass on the bank of the river.*

estuary–a place where a river meets the ocean. *Freshwater and salt water mix in an estuary.*

gills–the part of an animal's body that helps it breathe under water. *A fish takes in oxygen through its gills.*

habitat–a place where a plant or animal naturally grows and lives. *A trout lives in a water habitat, such as a lake or stream.*

mammal–an animal with an internal skeleton and backbone that breathes air through lungs and feeds its young on milk. *A manatee is a mammal that lives in the water.*

mangrove–a tropical evergreen tree or shrub with lots of branches and roots that look like trunks. *The manatee swam in the mangrove forest.*

marine–having to do with the sea. *A whale is a marine animal.*

marsh–a soft, wet lowland often covered with water. *The frog sat on a rock in the marsh.*

shoreline–the line where land and water meet. *Big waves crashed on the shoreline.*

swamp–a wet, low area of land with trees growing in it. *The crocodile swam in the swamp.*

tide–the rise and fall of the ocean every 12 hours. *At high tide, ocean water covers the beach.*

tide pool–a water habitat along shoreline rocks that fills with water when the tide is high. *At low tide, the tide pool animals dry out in the sun.*

Think About It!

1. Name as many animals as you can that live in the ocean.

2. What are gills?

3. What kinds of animals live in a tide pool?

4. What is the difference between a salt marsh and a freshwater marsh?

5. How is a river formed?

The Story and You!

1. If you could be an animal and live in any of the habitats mentioned in the book, which habitat would you choose? Why?

2. If you could ask a whale a question, what would it be?

3. What do you think it would be like to live in a swamp?

4. Brainstorm how you could make a model of a tide pool. How could you show the rise and fall of the tide? What animals would you include?

5. Imagine that you are traveling in a boat from a mountain stream to the ocean. What kinds of things do you think you would see?